Ten Principles for New Principals

A Guide to Positive Action

Mark Joel

**Ten Principles for New Principals:
A Guide to Positive Action**

Published by Robin Fogarty & Associates, Ltd.
Chicago, IL   Santa Fe, NM
800.213.9246
robinfogarty@aol.com
http://www.robinfogarty.com

Publisher: Brian Pete
Executive Editor: Robin Fogarty
Cover Design: Lisa Wright
Editor: Dara Lee Howard
Proofreader: Dora Vickary
Production Coordinator: Tim Scott
Series Coordinator: Maple Ann Cervo

Printed in Australia
ISBN 0-9701665-9-1

09 08 07 06 05 04 03 02   10 9 8 7 6 5 4 3 2 1

Dedication

I dedicate this book to Judy, Jon, and Andrew who support me in all of my endeavors, in good times and bad, and who bring me back to earth to enjoy the pleasures of life.

Contents

Preface

I applaud your decision to become a school administrator. You have the opportunity to have a great influence on the students of your school. But, with the power to influence comes a great deal of responsibility.

When Robin Fogarty suggested that I share my thoughts of the "ten principles new principals need to succeed," I agreed to write this book. As I compiled my thoughts, I reflected on my past fourteen years as a school administrator and educator; I am happy to say that I still maintain that it is the best of all professions.

Now that you have joined the ranks of education's leadership, I urge you to take this opportunity to share the power and responsibility of your position with the teachers, students, and community with whom you work.

Enjoy the journey!

Acknowledgments

I want to acknowledge with gratitude these sources of influence on my professional and personal development: new administrators, for their enthusiasm, ideas, and determination; principals, for their support and mentoring; vice principals, who made me walk the talk; teachers, parents, and students, with whom I have shared my vision; the school system, which allowed me to practice my profession; my parents for always being there; and, finally, the team that encouraged me to grow continually.

Introduction

To be a school principal is to be a member of one of the oldest, most respected professions. Yet, the role of school principal is a vast and complex one. Most parents and many teachers will say that they could never do the principal's job.

The role is constantly evolving and seems to require new skills almost daily. Being a school principal is a leadership position that requires executive ability, visionary skills, and particularly, management skills. Principals need to read continually to update their professional skills because they may be the single most important educational change agent in their school. More important, principals are the people in charge of the nation's most sacred resource: its children, its future. The principal with principles will survive and thrive in this challenging career.

This book gives many practical tips for the practicing principal. As you read the book, use Figure 1 to create your own list of top ten tips to add to mine. Because this book is a "work in progress," it will be revised from time to time. Please share your insights by leaving your comments on the Robin Fogarty & Associates Web site: http://www.robinfogarty.com.

To get the most from this book, you might want to just read it through, cover to cover. Or, you might want to read and dialogue with a colleague or mentor. Another way to use this book is as a guide for monthly discussions with other new principals. The ten principles provide great fodder for fertile discussions.

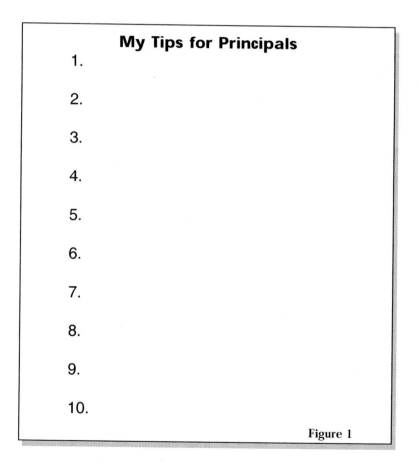

My Tips for Principals

1.

2.

3.

4.

5.

6.

7.

8.

9.

10.

Figure 1

Principle 1

Change Is Constant

Positive Action: **Know Where You Are Going; Know Why You Are Going There; and Know Who Is Going With You.**

There are a great many books on visionary leadership. They each present their own philosophical perspective, often accompanied by wonderfully quotable quotes. Yet, visionary leadership really boils down to a few specifics for principals as school leaders: vision, values, and visibility.

Vision: Know Where You Are Going

How do school principals know where they are supposed to go? Well, it's really more obvious than you think. One of the great truths is that there are many "constants" in education. Consider, for example, these remarks: Change is constant; financial and political accountability are here to stay; assessment continues to grow; and governance persists as an ongoing issue.

In individual school districts, educators often take these "constants" personally and feel they are somehow punitive in nature. The fact is, these "constants" are universal. When envisioning a course of direction, they must be part of the map. Reality is that things continue to change, financial and political accountabilities weigh heavily, student assessment grows, and governance is a constant issue.

As a principal deals with these "constants," his or her actions must be consistent with local board directions. The school principal is an executive of the school corporation and the CEO of the school building. As an executive with this corporation, a principal's job includes being in step with the strategic direction of the organization. However, this does not mean that the administrator is a corporate clone. Board policies are the guiding principles or the "roads on the road map" that need to be considered as the journey is charted. These policies affect finances, politics, and governance. Board policies often reflect the culture of the community, an area in which many administrators, particularly new ones, may stumble. They usually have a good understanding of the corporate culture (or they wouldn't have been promoted), yet they may fail to take the pulse of the community before changes are made. Although general principles, such as improving academic achievement and providing safe environments, are frequently the same, many social factors of "the community/neighborhood culture" can be significantly different between schools.

For example, a district may have schools in rural areas, high-density urban areas, established areas, and areas of great ethnic diversity. One needs to be aware of the cultural differences within the district (cultural as in a school culture sense, not an ethnic sense) when identifying the roads on the road map.

It's often a good idea to meet and greet the people of the school area and to follow the adage, "Stop, look, and listen before speaking." When principals understand the influence of the various cultural forces that may affect their vision or direction, they are more ready to incorporate these values into the implementation plan.

Values: Know Why You Are Going There

Values are the foundations from which principals operate within the corporate and community culture. Values are developed from family background, education, personal and professional readings, and the sum total of one's life experiences. Values are the "things" principals stand for—their bottom line! As such, it is important that these values are well articulated. Others can't be expected to know automatically what they are; the principal must share his or her values both explicitly and implicitly.

> **Values are the "things" principals stand for—their bottom line.**

When entering a new school, consider giving to each staff member and influential community member a small package that includes brief statements of your expectations about discipline, programs, parental involvement, teamwork, extracurricular activities, evaluation, and welcoming schools. It's important that the whole school community embraces these concepts. Then, post them in the office to ensure that decisions are consistent with the belief statements. This fosters accountability for the principal.

Visibility: Know Who Is Going With You

With vision and values in line, it is now time to walk the talk. Show students, teachers, and the community who is doing the driving and look for those who are willing to ride along. Being visible is essential for school administrators. With all of the paperwork, reports, and meetings that are part of normal school operations, it's easy to spend the day in the office doing these chores. That's why it's important to develop effective strategies that allow the principal to free up time for the truly important task of being visible, accessible, and available.

What is visibility? For sure, it is not simply gate keeping or being the protector of the building. Visibility means a number of things. It means at least one of the administration team is in the halls and in the yard during periods of transition; it means talking with parents in the yard, parking lots, and halls; it means knowing students by name and talking to them about their work, their role on a team, or their part in a performance; and finally, it means visiting classes and observing and talking with teachers. Visibility is about taking a personal and professional interest in the life of the school, all the time.

Why is visibility so important? Because it is the principal's lifeline, his or her connection to reality. Credibility with parents increases substantially when they call to question an action in the yard or classroom and the administrator already knows the facts and has been proactive in solving the problem. On-task behavior for all improves with the principal's presence. Vandalism and violence decrease as visibility increases because visibility shows that the principal cares enough to invest time.

By investing time in the present, principals gain the advantage in the future because there are fewer problems with parents, staff, and students. The principal's visibility, or lack of it, sets the tone for the school. This is probably one of the easiest tools administrators have at their disposal and it's also one of the most effective. When principals demonstrate to a school community who's doing the driving, they earn the respect of that community.

A Principalship Is a Political Position

Positive Action: **Don't Play the Politics.**

The position of principal is a political position, but one in which it is best not to play the politics. This may seem like a paradox but let me explain. The principal has many masters including students, staff, support staff, parents, the board administration, the board, and the community. It is this plethora of masters that makes the position so political. A principal blends two roles—senior executive and school representative—to succeed in performing a political job without being political.

> **A principal blends two roles—senior executive and school representative—to succeed in performing a political job without being political.**

Senior Executive

As a senior executive in the corporation, the school administrator must be aware of board policies and procedures and the politics of the system to ensure the greatest return for the students. This is being politically astute, which is significantly different from playing the politics.

School Representative

The administrator must keep the students and goals of the school at the forefront and use these as the focus for decision making. Principals have a responsibility to represent their schools and to strive for improvements.

Problems arise when principals play the politics in dealing with conflicting viewpoints. They run into difficulty when their personal opinions override their professional responsibilities, or when they side with one party or the other. Or worse, and what often occurs, principals try to side with all parties.

The danger in taking sides in a dispute is that the outcome moves from win–win to win–lose. Often, it is the administrator who loses, sometimes long after the original issue has been put to rest. By keeping the goals of students and school at the center of all decision making, a principal's credibility is never at stake.

In addition, it is important for principals to be clear on their position, so they don't appear weak or indecisive. Yet, they must not be personally attached to the situation or they lose credibility.

Finally, it seems wise to mention a common and particularly damaging mistake some administrators make by pitting one group against another. For example, using the school council to attack the board after the board turns down a request the principal has made. These actions inevitably become known, and, when they do, the credibility of the administrator suffers in the eyes of both school council and school board members.

Principle 3

First Impressions Are Lasting Impressions

Positive Action: **Think It Through! Do It Right!**

A school community gets first impressions in several ways: from the principal, from the school grounds and physical plant, and from the way they are treated during visits to the school.

Principals

Because new principals take on the role of the new kid on the block, people are trying to find out who they are, how they operate, and if they say what they mean and/or mean what they say.

> . . .there is only one chance to make a first impression. Make the best of it!

As everyone knows, there is only one chance to make a first impression. Make the best of it! Figure 2 shows a few tips for creating good first impressions. They include things like learning about the staff, being visible, greeting people sincerely, knowing names, and having an open door policy. This is a good time to be positive so people have something to believe in.

Tips for Creating Good First Impressions

1. Learn some personal information about each staff member before you arrive. Use it skillfully in your introductory meetings.

2. Be visible during transition times—in the halls, the yards, and the bus loop.

3. Greet people with a sincere smile and a firm handshake.

4. Learn as many names of students and parents as quickly as possible.

5. Have an "open door" policy for the principal's office.

Figure 2

School Grounds and Physical Plant

The school grounds and physical plant often create first, as well as continuing, impressions of a school. It is important for each principal to know what impression he or she wants people to take away as they drive or walk by or as they enter the yard or the building.

The vast majority of people in a school's community never enter the school. They base their opinion of the school on how it looks from the outside. They judge the book by its cover! Thus, it's critical to assess what they see. Is the playground litter free? Are there gardens? Do they look like gardens? How does the playground equipment look? Is the school painted? Are the signs inviting? These small things create the big picture and are critical in gaining the support of the outside community. Consider creating a team with community members to monitor these outward signs of excellence. What a terrific way to get the community involved with the school!

Treatment of Visitors to the School

When people enter the school, what is the first impression they get? Do they see students' work neatly displayed? Do they feel and see the instructional activity going on? More important, are they greeted warmly?

A trick I learned early is to post signs at all entrances of the school, stating that "Parents are always welcome in this school." All staff members are asked to acknowledge parents if they pass them in the halls. Saying "Good morning" or "May I help you?" creates a warm welcome and often puts parents at ease. It is important for the school administrative team, principal, vice principal, and clerical staff to model this. Staff members quickly take their cues from the principal's behavior.

Another good policy is to address people by name— this is such a big hit. It is truly amazing how few parents complain when they feel that school personnel take a personal interest in their child and display it by knowing a child's name.

Yet, a major concern for many school administrators is how to blend welcoming manners with safety concerns for the students. Yes, a safe school can be a welcoming school! The paradox of having a welcoming environment and at the same time, a safe school has always been there. However, as with most things, communication is the key. Welcome people and at the same time remind them to check in at the office. Encourage them to volunteer and have special identification for them so all are aware of their official role.

Parents are happy to comply when they know that the safety of the students, including theirs, is the concern being addressed. A school does not have to be cold and prison-like to be safe. Parents will think of the school as very welcoming when it is considered safe, yet friendly.

What is truly needed is the key called communication. Communication includes sending and receiving information. When sending information, principals want people to know both the rules of the school for school safety and that they are welcome to come to school. In receiving information, principals need to understand people's values, what concerns they have, and what they need in order to have a safe, welcoming environment.

A particularly good way to ensure that the princpal's vision of a positive impression is acheived is to enlist the assistance of both insiders and outsiders to develop a welcoming and safe school environment. As mentioned earlier, every school needs a school improvement team of interested parties whose purpose is to create a better environment for students, teachers, and parents. Its motto might be "Positive solutions for positive change." This team might include school council members, local police representatives, parents, teachers, administrative staff, and perhaps, students. The team needs both a clear mandate and precise knowledge of the range of their responsibilities and authority. Their task is not to take over the school or to do the job of the administration, but rather to help make the school a better place for all.

To be effective, a local group needs several things: to know who decides, that is, who has decision-making power for each part of the process; how big the sandbox is; and the freedom to work autonomously within this defined framework.

One word of caution! Nothing hurts this process more than having the group collaborate, decide, and then have the decision overturned by the administration. The principal must give a clear mandate and, then, let the team go! Tapping into the culture of a school community through the influence of a school improvement team is the foundation on which all future building will take place. After all, a good "building" needs a good foundation!

Principle 4

All Things Are Not Created Equal

Positive Action: **Manage Your Time or the Time Will Manage You.**

Every school district has a systemic plan of some sort. It is important for principals to have a basic understanding of the plan to ensure they move in the same direction as the policy. In addition to an overall plan, each district has a "current focus," whether it is assessment, safe schools, inclusive education, or technology. Understanding the current initiative and determining where it fits into the school plan will make life more manageable. Yet, often, just when a principal thinks that he or she has mastered the initiative, the initiative changes.

However, there are some things principals can do to help them keep the focus on long-term goals and at the same time, skillfully manage impending initiatives. These include knowing board policy, making choices, and managing time.

Knowing Board Policies

For a new principal, a working knowledge of the basic procedures of the district makes life more comfortable. Knowing the board's stand on discipline, evaluation, staffing, volunteers, split grades, and transportation makes a principal's decision making easier. These often are the very issues on which parents challenge a principal's choices.

Making Choices

Just as new teachers want to be liked by their students, new principals often want to make everyone happy. They make decisions that seem correct or convenient, but may not follow the procedures. These choices set a dangerous precedent.

Coloroso (1995) talks about three types of people: the jellyfish, the brick wall, and those with backbone. The same analogy can apply to school administrators. The jelly fish is the administrator who cannot or will not make a decision. When the going gets tough, jelly fish get lost! Their decisions are made by pressure and popularity. This style is dangerous because in their efforts to appease everyone, their inconsistency in decision making does not provide clear direction for the school.

Brick wall administrators have no flexibility and are often insecure with their authority and any challenges to it. They make decisions, right or wrong, and stick to them. These administrators are predictable but not very effective, and perhaps, not very likeable.

The third type is the administrator with backbone, who makes fair and consistent decisions based on principles and values. Their decisions are based in the procedures yet are flexible and able to accommodate the needs of an individual circumstance. For many new administrators, experience helps move them from jellyfish or brick wall to the administrator with backbone.

An administrator with backbone is incredibly important in times of change, and it is always a time of change. Consider developing a school handbook that reflects school procedures. Using a collaborative manner with input from teachers, students, and parents for the handbook helps create "buy in" to the policies.

Managing Time

Another important factor to deal with in the operations of a school is time management. Time is a priority resource, and a principal's time must be carefully managed.

Focus techniques for managing time are shown in Figure 3.

Time Management Focus Techniques

Use technology as a tool.

Touch paper once.

Decide who needs to do what.

Determine how much time something deserves.

Review the year at a glance.

Figure 3

Use Technology as a Tool

Use technology to make the job easier and more efficient. But, when its use is creating more work, get rid of it. Don't be a slave to technology! For example, most new school administrators enter their new job with good practical computer skills; the trick is

18   *Ten Principles for New Principals: A Guide to Positive Action*

becoming accustomed to the new programs. As any craftsman will tell you, good tools make a task easier, so it is important that the programs are good ones and suit the purposes for which they are being used. As with any new task, it's important to learn and practice the new skills until the task becomes routine. Give the programs a chance but if they don't work for you, try others. Make technology a plus, not a minus, in getting the job done.

Touch Paper Once

Handling a piece of paper once is a universal time management tip. Don't let the paperwork pile up; if it does, the job of handling it then seems enormous. Use several short periods during the day for paperwork. Quality time not quantity time is the key. Develop a system for reviewing paperwork. Look at a piece of paper and quickly determine if it is something that needs to be dealt with, and if so, whether you, the principal, or someone else should do it. If you, the principal, are going to do it, and it is urgent, deal with it immediately. If the topic is important but not urgent, add it to your work plan in accordance with its importance. For example, staffing or budget requirements are definitely more important that making most purchasing decisions or completing a survey. If someone else is going to deal with the topic, write a few notes of your expectations, due dates, and so on, and pass it to the responsible person.

Decide Who Needs to Do What

Delegating tasks is an important skill for a school administrator. It is important for an administrator's survival but is also important for other administration staff to have opportunities to develop their leadership and management skills. A mistake some new administrators make is in their belief that only they are capable of completing a task. They hoard the tasks and, consequently, become overwhelmed by the workload, spending more time on paperwork than on the more important people aspects of the job. In many cases, giving simple directions allows others to do the job. And, they may do it even better than you might!

Determine How Much Time Something Deserves

All tasks are not created equal! Even if they come from the district office, much of the paperwork that arrives is from a department seeking information, usually to be compiled in a report. Set priorities for responding to these requests. Analyze the report and determine who wants the information, how much information they want, when they want it, and what form the information should take. A school plan, an action plan, or an improvement plan all require major input and will need a major amount of scheduled work time to complete accurately and properly. However, many requests are for survey information and can be handled in a minimal amount of time.

Lay Out a Year at a Time

It is crucial to plan time for the important so that you are not consumed by the urgent.

Although the day-to-day events of a school administrator are unpredictable, there are many aspects of the job that are as predictable as the seasons. Certain tasks come around year after year, and during the same month. Setting up a year-long calendar and completing the predictable tasks ahead of time allows a principal to deal with the day-to-day crises in a less stressed manner.

Many administrators admit to being overwhelmed by the workload. Often, not always, this feeling results from a lack of long-range planning. They leave routine tasks until the last minute, then, when one of those day-to-day crises or events happen, they fall further behind, causing themselves more stress. It is crucial to plan time for the important so that you are not consumed by the urgent. Figure 4 briefly recaps a long-range plan with the major focus for each month. It serves as a template for new principals to use.

August

This is the month to start getting ready for the fall. Prepare now to ensure that support is available when the staff arrives. Cover timetable changes, room assignments, duty schedules, final hiring, and anything else that can be thought of and handled in advance. Having these all done ahead of time makes a smooth start for the year.

September

The great thing about each school year is that it gives everyone a chance to renew and to start over with a clean slate. Expectations from parents, students, and staff are high. It is the principal's job to ensure that everyone enters this phase of the year optimistically. Just as taking off is the most significant and potentially most dangerous part of an airplane's flight, so is September in the school year's progress. Great caution and care must be taken during September to ensure and maintain a great start.

October

October is a progressive month. Students are making great strides forward, parents are optimistic, teachers are involved in curriculum development and program implementation, and school councils are starting to focus on their role for the year. This is the time for the school administrator to monitor and manage change in the school. Review all at-risk students to ensure that they are properly accommodated.

November

Be wary of November! Students are getting tired of the routine. Parents are starting to panic over student achievement, or lack thereof. Teachers are getting ready for first-term reports and they, too, are getting tired. Parent councils (PTAs) are looking closely at both what has happened and what the future holds. The days are getting shorter and so are the patience levels. This is a great time for a spirit builder! Hold a potluck or catered lunch, have a barbecue, or write notes of appreciation.

December

Be aware of the community. This is usually the time for first-term reports, parent conferences, and seasonal celebrations. Tensions usually peak just prior to the conferences. This is also a time when the principal has tough decisions to make regarding staff and students. For example, how to support at-risk students, what action plans to implement, or which student placements to change. To coin a phrase from Stephen Covey (1990, p. 204), this is a time to strive for "win-win." However, reality or perception may not always let that be the case.

After the reporting period, the school enters a second phase in which some form of seasonal celebration takes place. Now, it is important for the administrator to know the community to ensure that the appropriate amount of time and energy is spent on this activity.

As the month progresses, the mood becomes more festive, routines both at home and at school start to break down, and personal emotional levels of staff, students, and parents vary dramatically. It is essential for administrators to be on their highest level of alert.

January

This is the time to review everyone's expectations. Help people get refreshed, renewed, and ready for the return to routine. Although people may not be as optimistic as they were in September, they have a chance to make changes and get back on track. This is a good time to review all safety plans for handling winter storms and winter weather. Also, identify at-risk students and be sure to notify parents. This is a highly productive month—make the most of it.

February

February, like January, is a time of high productivity. Student achievement and modifications to program are everyone's focus. To avoid the February blahs, make sure that some spirit-building activities are built into the program. This is a high parent involvement month, similar to November. This month tests a principal's conflict resolution skills.

March

March is a reporting month in most districts. Teachers, parents, and students are focused on reports. Many districts offer a spring break in this month.

April

April is the time to polish planning for the end of this year and to begin planning for next year. Update parents of at-risk students of plans for the end of the year. Start planning for budget forecasts, staffing issues, and school improvement plans for next year. As the school administrator, look two steps ahead.

May

Complete staff appraisals and plan graduation. Start looking at class organizations for next year. Rough timetables can be developed. School improvement surveys need to be developed and completed. At the same time, this is the time to plan the celebrations of success of the past school year.

June

As is December, June is the best of times and the worst of times. Planning for end-of-the-year celebrations and accommodating changes for next year can be very taxing activities. Just a few of the jobs to be done: finish timetables, create class lists, look at the total school organization, and hire new staff. All of these come at a time when the routines of staff and students are starting to wane.

July

Congratulate yourself! You have just completed your first full year as principal. You are exhausted, proud, and no longer a rookie. Keep smiling and go on holidays. Renew, relax, refresh—and come back to begin again!

Year at a Glance	
August	Prepare entry materials for fall.
September	Establish and enforce new routines.
October	Monitor and manage change.
November	Prepare for parent/teacher/student routine slump with informal event.
December	Confer with teachers and parents about tough decisions.
January	Review, renew, and start the year again.
February	Gear up for parental involvement.
March	Test and report, then enjoy spring break.
April	Start planning for next year.
May	Complete staff appraisals and plan graduation.
June	Clear final details and celebrate.
July	Go on holiday and replenish your energies.

Figure 4

Allow Other Lights to Shine

Positive Action: **Give Away the Power.**

It takes a great deal of work and trust to form a team. A team is not just a group of people working in the same building. Most teams are built over time with each piece of the team being built to fit. Teams are going to grow through many stages and not all of them are going to be positive. It is important for the leaders of the team to maintain confidence during turbulent times. Working and understanding the mission of the team is important. Developing this mission shares ideals, values, and principles. Trust is developed through the creation of a safe environment that maintains the integrity of the vision and personnel. Figure 5 shows five ways for creating cooperative, supportive teams of staff and teachers.

Team Building

Hire the best.

Support and mentor new teachers.

Develop a positive and caring environment.

Arrange a comfortable and inviting staff room.

Give away power.

Figure 5

Hire The Best

The principal is responsible to all to hire well.

The hiring of a new teacher is a multimillion dollar decision (35 years times the average salary plus benefits and pension). If the intangible cost to students or the actual cost of documentation, dismissal, and lawsuits are included, the impact of a poor hiring decision can be many times those millions. The principal is responsible to all to hire well. Here are some important tips, highlighted in Figure 6, for successful hiring.

Know what you want for the position. Know the personal, professional, and extracurricular skills required by the job. Make these the focus of the search.

Create a search team of at least three people, preferably with one person who is willing to disagree with you.

Do your homework. Check all references carefully. Know which of your colleagues you can trust for truthful references.

Craft your interview questions carefully. Know the human rights pitfalls, be aware of the types of questions that are legal to ask, and don't ask anything inappropriate.

Review an applicant's past practices. Remember that the greatest indicator of future performance is past practice. If an applicant didn't do something before, it's unlikely that he or she will do it now.

Avoid hiring "just like me" people. A common mistake that hiring team members make is to hire people similar to themselves. This bias may lead to a missed candidate who is ideal for the needs of the students in the school. So, go for the whole package, not just the immediate need.

Look for people who can add to the school profile. Always pick the best person in the draft. Very few people teach the same grade forever.

Keep notes for debriefing. All notes should be kept for at least one year after the interview. You may want to summarize the notes on each candidate.

Hiring Tips

Know what you want.

Create a team, including one person willing to disagree with you.

Do your homework.

Craft your interview questions carefully.

Review an applicant's past practices.

Avoid hiring "just like me" people.

Look for people who can add to the school profile.

Keep notes for debriefing.

Figure 6

Support and Mentor New Teachers

Providing ongoing support and mentoring for new teachers is a great responsibility for school administrators. Most new teachers who leave the profession do so because they feel isolated. They have spent huge amounts of emotional energy but don't see a return for their expenditures. Setting up a mentoring program and carefully matching experienced teachers with new teachers provides a double-edged system. It gives new teachers a confidante and, at the same time, gives experienced teacher-mentors access to tips from the new graduate and the chance to articulate tried-and-true practices from the mentor's experience. This encourages personal reflection by both new teacher and mentor.

Develop a Positive and Caring Environment

There is a cartoon that says in effect "The firings will continue until morale improves." As many leaders have discovered, a positive and caring environment cannot be mandated. Work like a gardener—plant seeds (expectations) carefully and nurture them as they grow. Modeling expectations leads to the greatest impact on situations. The "Golden Rule" definitely applies: treat others in the building with the manners that you want them to use with you. State expectations so that people understand what is wanted. And, as any good gardener does, weed when necessary. But remember, to get rid of a few weeds doesn't require spraying the whole garden with herbicide.

Arrange a Comfortable and Inviting Staff Room

Is it a professional sanctuary or an exclusive club? What is the role of the staff room? Who should control it? Who is allowed in? What is allowed? Nothing seems to create more passionate responses from staff members than defining the role of the staff room. Many staff conflicts occur over seating arrangements, the visitor policy, and what topics of conversations are appropriate. Some principals avoid the staff room, but let's explore one fully developed view on staff rooms. Then, only you can say if the view is right or wrong for your situation. Figure 7 briefly suggests some policies for the staff room that have worked well.

Staff Room Guidelines

Stick to positive comments.

Do not post negative messages.

Welcome visitors.

Keep the room clean.

Make it comfortable.

Visit often as the principal.

Figure 7

Stick to Positive Comments

Comments in the staff room must be positive. No student, teacher, or parent name should be used in a negative manner. Although the staff room is a place where staff can relax, it is important not to allow the conversation to degenerate by having negative talk. Although this talk may be "just venting," if wrongly interpreted, it can easily poison staff and community relationships. Usually, it is sufficient to start with this policy and use a few reminders throughout the year to help the staff room maintain its profile as a professional lounge.

Do Not Post Negative Messages

No negative political or union messages may be posted. In most schools, the staff room has become public domain. Because volunteers may work in the space and with public access to the building after hours for community activities, the public may have direct access to information posted in the staff room. Keep it positive.

Welcome Visitors

Visitors are welcome. Coffee is provided by the office. Open the room to school volunteers so that they have an opportunity for a break. It is amazing the support the public gives to educators when they can identify with them as "real people."

Keep It Clean

A committee is formed to keep the room clean. A staff room can make even the messiest teenager's room look clean after a few short weeks. Establish a routine.

Make It Comfortable

The staff room should be comfortable. Teachers, staff, and volunteers work hard. They need a place to relax in order to continue being positive and upbeat with students. Ensure that their staff room is at least a partial oasis for them.

Visit Often as the Principal

School administrators should visit often to develop a pulse for the mood of their staffs. There are few opportunities for teachers to interact with the school administration. Having one of the administrators available at breaks or lunch allows teachers to discuss issues, professional or personal, with the administrator. Also, just having a member of the administration in the staff room ends negative conversations. It is my experience that the conversational tone changes, for the positive, within minutes of a principal's entrance.

Give Away the Power

It is easy to use power to say "No," but it is important to use power to say "Yes."

The school administrator is one of the few positions in the system in which one can actually give away power. This power energizes others and allows them to shine. School administrators who don't share their power often face burn out. The concept of sharing power is trying for many new administrators because they find it difficult to give away the decision-making role that they worked so hard to achieve. In reality, those who learn to delegate responsibly by defining parameters, cheerleading, and providing resources gain power and influence. Staff members and community come to realize that better decisions are being made and that their leader is a confident, self-assured person. It is easy to use power to say "No," but it is important to use power to say "Yes." Yes power enables others and leads to positive outcomes.

After curriculum leadership, human resource management is the most important job for a school administrator. The understanding and managing of the school improvement team, collective agreements, the support of school personal, and the interpersonal interaction with staff, students, and community are essential for an effective school.

Principle 6

People Share Their Interpretation of Your Message

Positive Action: **Help People Hear What You Say.**

The better the understanding parents and public have about what is happening in their school, the greater the level of commitment and support they will have toward the school. For many people, the only access to information about their schools and educational system is through articles written in the newspaper. These articles often involve negative incidents. Insiders to the school know there are other, positive stories as well and and they need to be shared with the community. Developing communication skills and a communication plan is critical.

Figure 8 reviews the communication tips.

Communication Tips		
Speaking	**Listening**	**Writing**
Confidence	Focus	Tone
Clarity	Rapport	Clarity
Sincerity	Reflection	Brevity
	Confirmation	Appearance
		Examples
		Accuracy
		Quality
		Figure 8

Speaking

A school administrator needs excellent communication skills, including confidence, clarity, and sincerity. The ability to speak to large groups of teachers, paraprofessionals, elected officials, or parents is essential.

Confidence

Administrators need to develop the confidence and presence to speak effectively. Heighten effectiveness by tailoring the language to the audience. Appropriate language helps an audience understand the school administrator's message. Remember, for an audience of non-educators, there is nothing worse than listening to educational jargon or "educationese."

Clarity

Good speakers also ensure that the main points of a message are clearly stated, and, often, repeated or graphically presented. They check for understanding through reflection or questioning, thus re-enforcing major points or topics. A lesson learned early is that people pass on their interpretation of your message. To avoid misinformation, when you make a statement, comment, or opinion, state it confidently and clearly. Give an example. Ask for clarifying questions.

Sincerity

For school administrators, how something is said is as important as what is said. Mastering the skills of words, nonverbal communication, and tone is critical. This is especially true during the peak traffic periods in the school: a half hour prior to morning bell until a half hour past, recesses, lunch, and after school.

During these periods, principals make 90% of their interpersonal contacts—teachers with a question, a problem in the yard, a bus incident, or a parent wanting just a few minutes of your time. Many times, this requires triage skills. For example, after dealing with a difficult parent and while still mulling over the situation, a principal is asked a question by a staff member. The principal unintentionally shows a lack of focus or uses a negative tone or negative body language, even though the principal would normally respond to that kind of question in a positive way.

Listening

Listening is an art unto itself. Stephen Covey (1990) identifies the habit of communication—Habit 5, "Seek first to understand, then to be understood." One of the key paradigms is, "If I listen first to understand, then I will be better understood."

> **Key listening strategies include focus, rapport, reflection, and confirmation.**

School administrators listen to many complaints, concerns, or problems. It is easy to develop the habit of jumping to conclusions, but try not to. Take the time to actively listen and reflect. This helps principals develop a good rapport with their public. In fact, the public responds by feeling that their concerns are taken seriously and adds to the administrator's credibility. Key listening strategies include focus, rapport, reflection, and confirmation.

Focus

Focus means "being there" and making sure that the speaker has the listener's undivided attention. The listener maintains eye contact in a nonthreatening way and avoids disruptions during the discussions.

Rapport

Rapport means establishing connection and comfort—putting the speaker at ease. Many people are still uncomfortable coming to a school or visiting the principal. As the principal and as a listener, try to put them at ease and lower their anxiety . . . and hostility levels. One technique that helps is to sit around a table instead of talking across a desk. Courteous administrators offer their visitors a chair, and maintain a calm manner at all times. This shows a sense of care and control.

Reflection

Reflection means that listeners rephrase or ask questions to ensure that they are clear about what they are hearing. Using these strategies leads to a point of conclusion. Always try to focus on the problem and a resolution to the problem that will be "Win–Win."

Confirmation

Confirmation means restating main points at the conclusion of a talk, because sometimes, during discussion, "the who does what" gets lost. Restating the action plan, including timelines, ensures that all parties take away the same understanding. A follow-up phone call adds a needed dose of "good will."

Writing

During the year, many pieces of written information are sent from school to home. How many and how much of these are read is the 64 million dollar question. A prediction is that, as with newspapers, the headlines and first few paragraphs of letters and newsletters are what the majority of people read. To accommodate that prediction, here are some guidelines for effective writing.

Positive Tone

Use positive headlines and a positive tone. Newsletters are a great place for praise! Highlight the great things that are happening at the school. Sports teams, music and drama presentations, and academic achievements are all things that the community likes to read about.

Clarity

Avoid educational jargon. The jargon and acronyms are difficult enough for people in the business of education and are totally foreign to the public. Using jargon in publications only creates another barrier between the public and school system.

Brevity

Keep the message brief, clear, and concise. Less is better. Many people read only headlines and the first few words of each article. They are more likely to read the whole article if it's brief.

Appearance

Keep the layout clean and the font clear. Use pictures and graphic, not words, to fill spaces. These make a newsletter more attractive and inviting.

Examples

Keep samples of good newsletters and other letters. Keep them on the computer. They can be great time savers as the principal is creating a new newsletter.

Accuracy

Have many people proofread the product. It is hard for writers to find their own mistakes. Even a few typos give the wrong impression to the reader. Make publications error free, or as close to that as a team can get. Spend extra time checking dates and locations. These errors, although not obvious to the writer's eye, are almost certain to come back to haunt you.

Quality

Remember that the final product reflects on you, the school, and the educational system. A few extra minutes invested in review pay big dividends.

Communication is the key to success. It is a learned skill that has to be practiced and monitored on a regular basis. Communicators need to be clear about what they want to communicate before they begin. It is equally important to know the intended audience. The method of communication—writing, speaking, or listening—must be appropriate for the situation. At all costs, avoid jargon. Messages must be honest and straight forward. Be considerate in delivery, recognize the tone being used, and be aware of nonverbal communication. It is important to have a communication plan complete with samples of exemplary letters and newsletters. Whatever form communication takes, principals need to respect themselves and their organization.

The Buck Stops Here

Positive Action: **Be Consistent! Be Flexible! Be There!**

It has been said that academic qualifications get you the job and interpersonal skills or the lack of them take you out of the job. If that is true for school administrators, they will want to pay close attention to the many decisions that are needed every hour of every day. To facilitate the decision-making process, there are a number of tips that may tame the process for those new at the game. See Figure 9 for a listing of these tips.

Attitude for Decision Making

Don't exaggerate the negative. Try for a balanced consideration of a problem. The brain cannot distinguish real from imagined—both kinds of thoughts appear similar. If negative thoughts are played over and over, the brain asks the body to respond to them as if they were real.

Find a comfortable problem-solving strategy and use it. One strategy is ICRIE, which stands for "Information, Consultation, Recommendations, Implementation, and Evaluation." For each situation, use these steps, mentally or in writing, to note the impact of the decision. Then, a decision maker can be confident that he or she has thoroughly handled the situation.

Don't own the problem if it is not yours to own! Help others—staff, students, and parents—by providing opportunities to capture the whole picture, express their concerns, and develop a resolution. Leaders do not have to compromise their integrity for others. Although principals should not allow others to suffer undo harassment, they do need to allow others to accept responsibility for their actions.

Try for a balanced consideration of a problem.

Follow up. It is not always possible for the principal to have a full understanding of each situation when faced with it. However, when a school administrator tells someone he or she will get back to them, he or she must do so in a timely manner.

Avoid absolute comments. Inevitably, school administrators may become frustrated with situations, and make statements that land them in hot water. For example, a principal might say to a student who is a chronic visitor, "The next time I see you at the office, you will be suspended." Well, this student does some silly little thing, ends up at the office, and presents the principal with a quandry—follow through on the action or back track. Following through means justifying to angry parents why the student has been suspended for a trivial matter. The moral of the story is to be absolute if necessary, but use care and try to think things through to avoid future situations.

Communicate. New principals might want to develop a network of colleagues to talk to about sticky situations. There are few problems that are new or original. Thus, a network of colleagues with a similar experience level might help with the concerns that come up. Talk to these people about lower level operational problems. But, also have experienced mentors with whom to discuss more serious situations. And, keep supervisors informed of any potentially explosive situations. Live the phrase, "No surprises."

Pay attention to the human factor. School administrators are in the people business. The human factor plays a huge part in every decision. The stresses of family for students, staff, and parents play a role in how a situation escalates. Being in tune to these situations allows a principal to make appropriate decisions and accommodate consequences. The principal needs to be aware of his or her patience level on any given day and to defer decisions when necessary, rather than making hasty decisions.

> **Live the phrase, "No surprises."**

Know legal responsibilities. It's important that school administrators have a good understanding of their role and responsibilities as outlined by government agencies. In particular, they need to understand the policies and procedures of the local school board, because the local board is the guiding light for their decisions. This may be especially true when handling new or difficult situations.

School administrators make many decisions every day, both big and small. They walk a fine line between over-thinking, over-analyzing, and over-reacting. Over time and with practice, principals gain confidence in their decision-making ability. Again, the backbone for everything a principal does is to have a clearly defined set of values. Using those values and acting reasonably and rationally usually produce sound decisions.

Making Good Decisions

Don't exaggerate the negative.

Find a comfortable problem-solving strategy and use it.

Don't own the problem if the problem isn't yours to own.

Follow up.

Avoid absolute comments.

Communicate.

Pay attention to the human factor.

Know legal responsibilities.

Figure 9

Together Is Better

Positive Action: **Invite Partnerships**

Developing links between business, education and communities is one of today's fundamental challenges. It is now more important than ever that we work together to address the complex challenge of changing the way we educate our learners. Co-operation between public and private sectors and community wide partnerships are critical to meet the needs of students and employers and, ultimately, to ensure prosperity and success for all. (Conference Board of Canada, 1996)

There has and will continue to be controversy about school/business partnerships. Fear of multinational corporations controlling the philosophical and ideological viewpoints of schools and creating corporate schools has been around since the beginning of corporate/school partnerships. The reality of funding cutbacks is that educators need to look at alternative forms of funding. Carefully planned and well-managed partnerships may provide the means to deliver more quality in education programs.

Before starting a partnership, it is imperative that principals are fully aware of the policies and procedures of their boards and of their communities' desires with regard to this matter. Failure to comply with these policies and wishes may lead to future difficulties.

How to Create Partnerships

It takes a number of actions in a number of different areas to create a partnership (Figure 10). Let's look at these actions, one by one.

Actions to Create Partnerships

Determine the need and establish a team.
Look for and approach a compatible partner.
Start with a clear vision of the partnership.
Create a strategic plan.
Set goals.
Establish limits of involvement.
Monitor activities.
Communicate.
Provide media coverage.
Be sensitive to political realities.
Avoid gimmicks.
Celebrate success.
Review need for partnership after completing project.

Figure 10

Need and Team

Determine the need for a partnership and establish a team comprised of school administrators, teachers, parents, and students. Then, have the team create and monitor the partnership plan with its members acting as gatekeepers.

Compatible Partners

Seek a compatible partner and approach them. Keep the focus on the school and students, and be sure all partners have a clear understanding from the beginning that the school and students are in the forefront of the partnership.

Vision of the Partnership

Start with a clear vision of what the partnership will look like. To be successful, partnerships must be win–win situations with clearly defined mutual benefits, and a vision shared by all participants.

Strategic Plan

Create a strategic plan. Develop a time line for implementation. Include in the plan a development phase in which goals are established, time lines are set, and resources and personnel are allocated. Let this plan become the basis of the implementation stage in which the action occurs. After implementation, review and execute the plan to ensure that the goals of the project and partners were met.

Goals

Set realistic goals in a collaborative manner. Although the major benefit of the partnership must be the good of the students, mutual benefit to all partners must also be present. By setting realistic goals collaboratively, all parties will be pleased with the progress and remain dedicated to the partnership.

Limits of Involvement

Clearly establish limits of involvement by setting boundaries. This lets each party know how they fit into the whole project. Often, because of too much enthusiasm at the start of a project, one partner may overstep a boundary, creating a situation that takes valuable time and resources to resolve. Try to avoid these dilemmas by setting clear parameters.

Monitoring

Monitor on a regular basis. Anything that is worth doing is worth keeping an eye on. Monitoring provides feedback for all parties and helps partners change the allocation of resources when necessary. It also provides opportunities to celebrate the successes.

Communicate regularly with all stakeholders in the partnership.

Communicating

Communicate regularly with all stakeholders in the partnership. There can never be too much communication. Communicate on expectations, progress, concerns, and celebrations.

Media Coverage

Provide media coverage. Not only do partners love to see their names in print, showing endorsement for them and their companies, but also schools need every bit of positive media coverage that they can get. This type of publicity shows the public that most schools are not in crisis, but rather are doing a fine job with the students.

Political Realities

Be sensitive to the political realities. Do not use a partnership to play politics. Know the limits of school board procedures and follow them. Remember, the purpose of the partnership is to enhance the educational goals of the district.

Gimmicks

Avoid blatant marketing schemes and gimmicks. Because education is a long-term business, educators need to ensure that their marketing strategies reflect the quality of the image that they wish to present. People remember negatives for a long time. Someone has said that it takes ten positives to erase the memory of one negative. Don't give the public that one negative to remember.

Celebration

Celebrate successes. Nothing encourages future participation by traditional or new partners like success. Everyone likes to back a winner. Celebrate and acknowledge all who participated.

After Action Review

Review the need for the partnership after the project has been completed. As with any implementation project, take time to review and reflect before beginning the next phase. If the project is benefiting the students, staff, community, and partners, then continue. If not, then it is time to part ways as friends.

Attitude

As with setting a "welcoming school" environment, the principal's attitude is the key factor in partnership successes. Not every partnership is a big one. Some of the best partnerships are with local parents. For example, the principal of one school encountered a group of parents who were interested in helping to raise students' reading scores. These parents established a home reading program, based on incentives for participation. The parents offered their time to establish the program and monitor progress. The school offered materials to read, support from the staff to collect sheets at the beginning of class, and space in the newsletters to promote and celebrate the program. This program had parents working with staff and parents working with kids. Community stores provided the celebrations. The results were that students' reading scores improved. Parents, teachers, and students had a better sense of community. This project tapped parents' potential in a positive way. It turned a potentially negative situation in which parents were upset with reading test scores into a positive experience and relationship. If the principal had not allowed parents to contribute in a positive way, they might have had negative thoughts about the school. On a side note, although the school improved through this partnership, the workload for the principal did not increase.

With a little imagination, there are many opportunities for partnerships in a school. It is important that administrators know their board procedures and follow them. Involve the parents and community, and get them on board. Have a clear vision of the project and establish working boundaries for the project. And celebrate success!

Principle 9

Accountability Counts

Positive Action: **Start Counting!**
Keep Counting

Does teaching drive accountability or does accountability drive teaching? This is the question of the day. Nothing drives schools, districts, parents, teachers, and school administrators into a frenzy faster that the approaching release of test scores. High scores equate to more money, more freedom, and more support from the community and, unfortunately, lower scores cause an equal but negative spiral of effects.

In the end, if educators create effective schools, build strong learning communities, and provide an effective leadership environment, they will no longer be victims of the "test syndrome." So, how does one lead for success? Let's analyze this idea further. See Figure 11 for a review of a notable seven-step process of leadership (Lezotte, 2001).

How to Lead for Success

There has been much research on what makes schools effective. Lezotte's (2001) seven components probably represent the best and most comprehensive approach. These seven steps include:

If something is worth doing, it is worth monitoring.

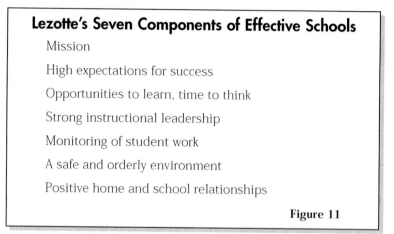

Lezotte's Seven Components of Effective Schools

Mission

High expectations for success

Opportunities to learn, time to think

Strong instructional leadership

Monitoring of student work

A safe and orderly environment

Positive home and school relationships

Figure 11

Having a clear and focused mission. This is what a good leader brings to the team. Although a leader is not solely responsible for this, the leader is responsible for creating an environment for a clear mission to develop. Once in place, decisions are based on their relation to this mission.

Establishing high expectations for success. It is essential that leaders know what is wanted. Expectations need to be attainable; resources, human and financial, must be allocated to the situation. High expectations yield high results.

Creating opportunities to learn. Learning is what schools are all about. If educators don't create the opportunities and keep improving on them, then they will get what they always get, and improvement will not occur as it should.

Having strong instructional leadership. There are many studies on the implications of leadership on test scores. All indicate that strong leadership is essential for success. The leader sets the tone, establishes the guidelines for success, and ensures that these guidelines are followed.

Frequently monitoring student progress. If something is worth doing, it is worth monitoring. Feedback provides the catalyst for continued growth and improvement. The monitoring of student progress provides the teacher with feedback on the effectiveness of the teaching strategies used. This feedback loop is needed for continued improvement through appropriate adjustments and modifications.

Strong leadership is shared leadership.

Having a safe and orderly environment. The optimal learning environment allows teachers to teach and students to learn . . . without distractions. It instills confidence in parents and the community that the school is in good shape and that learning is going on.

Having strong home and school relationships. When these relationships are nurtured, that is, when the parents support the work of the teachers and the teachers respect the role of the parents, the outcome for the students is bound to be positive because both parents and school are focused on providing quality education for the students.

Each component in the leadership equation has to be addressed in a systematic way and must remain the driving force for everything that schools do. The components must be discussed frequently and cultivated carefully. Then, in that way, accountability for an "effective school" is focused on the learning environment for leadership and curriculum.

Creating a Learning Environment

To create a learning environment, one has to model it. Staff members take their cue from the principal. There should be evidence on a consistent basis of people learning. What does this look like? It looks like staff development as part of every staff meeting; activities that are not too long or onerous; the sharing of ideas, articles; and reporting about a conference recently attended. Also, in creating a learning environment, professional reading materials are available in the staff room. Attendance at conferences is encouraged and funded wherever possible. A parent bulletin board might display articles relevant to parents and their children. Parent discussion groups are facilitated. With all of this active modeling of learning, staff and students are bound to catch some of it!

Strong Leadership/Shared Leadership

Strong leadership is shared leadership. The role of the principal is to bring out the best in everyone else. This means that the school administrative team establishes the boundaries and climate necessary for success. Then, each individual or group has the freedom to operate within these parameters in order to create a successful environment.

This technique allows the best education for both students and parents and gives teachers and support personnel the creative freedom to meet the challenge of providing a great educational environment.

Changing Curriculum

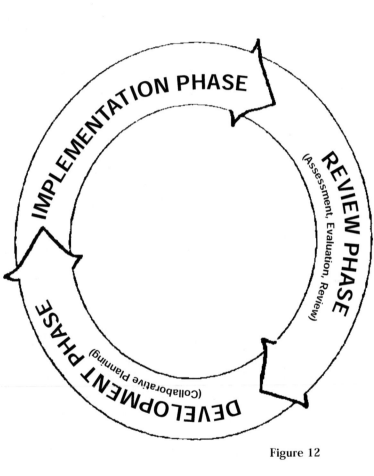

Figure 12

One of the most useful tools for a new school principal is the Curriculum Review, Development, and Implementation (CRDI) model (Figure 12). This model can be the basis for all new curriculum implementation. It should come as no surprise that the model promotes review, development, and implementation.

Review

This stage is the stage of analysis and includes a number of things, beginning with creating a committee to look at the curriculum to be implemented. The committee determines, by using gap analysis, if changes need to take place. It looks at the desired outcomes and determines which practices should remain the same and which need to be changed. It reviews current learning materials and resources and determines which are appropriate and examines new materials that may need to be added.

Development

This stage is the stage of creating the model. A plan is created that includes timelines, costs, key players, a list of materials that need to be developed, and the sites of staff development activities. This is the phase in which creative energies flow, and plans are articulated in as much detail as possible.

Implementation

This stage is the stage of change and is the actual process of going from the present to the future. Successful implementation requires all parties see the need for the change, have the time required to successfully change, and provide the support and resources to implement the initiative. Participants need to be aware that problems and obstacles may pop up from time to time and will have to be dealt with. They also need to know that having some vocal resistors among the group is okay. Resistors help articulate the values and beliefs of the group, and, in the end, create a more effective product.

> **Resistors help articulate the values and beliefs of the group. . .**

It is critical to implement only a reasonable number of changes at one time. Michael Fullan talks about the "implementation dip." No, the "dip" is not the principal, but rather the process by which things may get worse before they get better. At this stage, it is very important that the staff be aware of the administration's support and dedication to the change.

It's also important to take time to celebrate the success of the change and to enjoy the process. Remember, what doesn't kill us makes us stronger!

Principle 10

Work Smarter
Positive Action: **Prioritize! Prioritize! Prioritize!**

The job of school administrator is never ending. For each principal, there is a beginning—the day that he or she enters the building—and there is an ending—the day he or she leaves and someone else takes over. But, the cycle continues for that someone else. There are some key elements to consider in terms of the principal's work habits.

Working

If a principal thinks that staying just a "little longer" will make things better, that principal may not succeed. In limited circumstances, longer and harder work pays off, but if this mode of work is the rule for a person, it may only make things worse. The economic concept called marginal productivity directly addresses this issue. Marginal productivity relates productivity, time, and effort on a continuum. Simply put, this continuum shows that productivity increases with time/effort until a certain point, after which gains in productivity start to decrease and become negative. This effect can snowball if workers are tired, frustrated, and not refreshed. They can actually begin the day less productively than the previous day or run out of energy earlier than before. In school settings, it is easy to observe this effect for both teachers and administrators as the term progresses. What does this mean? It means that by working longer, one may actually be doing less. The phrase "smarter, not harder" applies here.

Prioritizing

"Working smarter, not harder or longer" does not mean that one can do little and get by. It means that principals have to learn to prioritize. Prioritizing means to distinguish between jobs that are urgent and those that are important, and then to spend the appropriate amount of time and energy on each. If administrators spend all their time on the urgent, they will never get to the important. If they avoid the urgent, then chaos occurs, and they do not have time for the important because they are busy cleaning up messes. Determining the priority of each job and the appropriate amount of time for each is the key here.

Delegating

Delegation is a skill that has to be learned. Simply giving a job to a person or group and then redoing their work after it has been completed is not successful delegation. It doubles the delegator's work and demoralizes the staff. Rather, delegate by outlining expectations, setting time expectations, and supporting the group. Assign initial projects and understand that they may not be up to standards at first but with time and coaching they can improve. It's important to remember that delegating frees the delegator to do other urgent or important tasks. In the end, delegating fosters a group leadership base and a collaborative environment for the school.

Attitude is everything—only you can control yours.

Personal Resiliency

Dick O'Brien is a motivational speaker on the subject of personal resiliency and wellness, both important issues for any administrator. A new principal benefits from developing skills in personal control and attitude. O'Brien's key points (2001), shown in Figure 13, are briefly presented for consideration by the new leader.

> **You chose this job of principal. Enjoy it.**

O'Brien's Key Points for Personal Resiliency

Attitude

Responding

Negativism

Personal places

Change

Successes and defeats

Owning the day

Body signals

Sense of humor

Figure 13

Attitude

Attitude is everything—only you can control yours. When waking up in the morning, choose how your day is going to go. Choose to start the day in a positive way. Set routines that allow you to be the best that you can be. Your response to the many challenges that occur throughout the day determines whether you allow these responses to create a bad day.

Responding

Learn to respond rather than react. As a new principal, this may be difficult at first because you try to be all things to all people. Practice. Practice. Practice. Your responses create impressions on those you influence. When they see you respond in a reasonable, consistent, and predictable manner, this establishes a pattern for their behavior, too.

Negativism

Rise above the negative. A principal sets the tone for the building. If a principal doesn't rise above the negative influences, how can he or she expect the staff to be positive? You chose this job of principal. Enjoy it.

Don't exaggerate the negative—95% of the worries will not come true. Brain theory tells us that our brains do not differentiate between what is real and what is perceived. Playing negative thoughts over and over leads to actually thinking something negative is happening and sets body reactions accordingly. By practicing positive self-thoughts, for example, that a parent coming in about a problem will be reasonable, is a better way to approach the principalship. For that other 5% of the worries that do come true, worrying does not help one deal with them in a systematic way. Deal with them, yes, but control the worrying.

Personal Places

Develop personal fall backs, private retreats, and sacred places. Make these your anchors, and devote time to them. Unless the urgent is an emergency, urgent matters should not be allowed to interfere with this time. Take a few minutes each day to engage in a stress releasing activity.

Change

Become a change expert. Change is ongoing. That is life. Learn to deal with it in a positive way. There are many great books on change; take time to read some. Although the rate of change in knowledge and technology is mind boggling, it's clear that change is going to continue. Learn to manage change so that change doesn't manage you.

Successes and Defeats

Celebrate successes and learn from (but minimize) defeats. In the education business, principals are often favorite targets. People criticize their hours, their holidays, and the perception of wonderful working conditions. Everyone who ever went to school figures he or she is an expert on schools. Celebrations of successes are a needed part of the principalship.

Owning the Day

Take ownership of your day before leaving home. If you are disorganized and out of sorts before you get to the office, don't expect things to get better when you get there. And, the same is true when you go home. Try to leave home problems at home and work problems at work. It sounds so simple, and it is when you work at it.

Body Signals

Be aware of your body signals and respond appropriately. "We are dying from the way we live." Be aware of what you are doing to your body. Balance food, drink, exercise, and relaxation. Bodies give signs when they are reaching their limits. Learn to recognize these signs and react accordingly. Ignoring them may be dangerous to your life.

Sense of Humor

A successful leader never loses his or her sense of humor. Laughter is a great tool in the building of personal resiliency. Humor acts as a buffer against stress. Many stress patients take life too seriously, letting negative thoughts invade and dominate their mental well-being. If one keeps a proper perspective on each event and learns to laugh at him- or herself, he or she finds that others follow suit and do the same. School becomes a more pleasant and productive place.

Mentoring

Schools are entering a period of massive administration change. Today, because of the increasing shortages, many people are becoming principals with minimal teaching and administrative experience. At the same time, there are few experienced people to approach for advice. Because of early retirement incentives, the baby boomers are surging into retirement and fewer candidates aspire to principalships.

Because there are fewer experienced administrators to call on, it is important that a new principal get involved in a cohort mentor group. This is a group of administrators with like experience who are supported by a seasoned administrator. The group meets regularly to discuss both the positives and the negatives of their individual situations. Members are supportive and willing to share. By sharing, the group's collective results often are substantially better than the individual's results. Also, by sharing these concerns, each new principal realizes that he or she is not alone and that others face the same or similar problems, which reduces stress.

In the past, mentor groups happened naturally when a group of teachers became administrators, and they progressed as before. However, with the rapid change and mobility of administrators, it is essential to establish these groups in a more formal manner.

Personal resiliency is a key to a successful career in administration. Principals need to accept that change is ongoing, that they alone are responsible for their attitudes, that they have control of their lives, that their ongoing learning is important to working smarter, and that they need to take time to reflect on their successes. In addition, they need to be aware of their body signals and attend to them. After all, not only do these individuals want to be principals but they also have taken courses, worked on committees, and gathered the support of their senior administration to get the job; now, let them enjoy it! Let each be a Principal with principles!

Let each be a principal with principles!

Bibliography

Principle 1: Change Is Constant

Positive Action: Know Where You Are Going; Know Why You Are Going There; and Know Who's Going With You.

Dufour, R. (1998). *Professional learning communities at work*. Alexandria, VA: Association for Supervision and Curriculum Development.

Senge, P. (1999). *The dance of change*. New York: Doubleday.

Senge, P. (2000). *Schools that learn*. New York: Doubleday.

Principle 2: Leadership Is a Political Position

Positive Action: Don't Play the Politics.

Deal, T., & Peterson, K. (1999). *Shaping school culture*. San Francisco: Jossey-Bass.

Hargraves, A., & Fullen, M. (1998). *What's worth fighting for out there?* Mississauga, Ontario, Canada: Ontario Public School Teachers Federation.

Principle 3: First Impressions Are Lasting Impressions

Positive Action: Think It Through! Do It Right!

Boothman, N. (1999). *How to make people like you in 90 seconds or less*. Kendall, Canada: Fleetwood Press.

Goleman, D. (1995). *Emotional intelligence: Why it can matter more than IQ*. New York: Bantam Books.

Greenleaf, R. (1991). *Servant leadership*. New York: Paulist Press.

Principle 4: All Things Are Not Created Equal

Positive Action: Mange Your Time or The Time Will Manage You!

Banchard,K. (1982). *The one minute manager.* New York: Berkley Publishing Group.

Carlson, R. (1998). *Don't sweat the small stuff.* New York: Hyperion.

Coloroso, B. (1995). *Kids are worth it.* Toronto, Ontario, Canada: Somerville House Publishing.

Covey, S. (1990). *The seven habits of highly effective people.* New York: Simon and Schuster.

Daresh, J., & Playko, M. (1997). *Beginning the principalship - A practical guide for new school leaders.* Thousand Oaks, CA: Corwin Press.

Principle 5: Allow Other Lights to Shine.

Positive Action: Give Away the Power!

Blase, J., & Kirby, P. (1999). *Bring out the best in teachers.* Thousand Oaks, CA: Corwin Press.

Fogarty, R. (2001). *Ten things new teachers need to succeed.* Arlington Heights, IL: Skylight Professional Development.

Kolbe, K. (1990). *The conative connection.* New York: Addison Wesley.

Lambert, L. (1998). *Building leadership capacity in schools.* Alexandria, VA: Association for Supervision and Curriculum Development.

Principle 6: People Share Their Interpretation of Your Message

Positive Action: Help People Hear What You Say!

Bolton, R. (1979). *People skills.* New York: Simon and Schuster.

Bozek, P. (1991). *50 one minute tips to better communication.* Menlo Park, CA: Crisp Publications.

Burley-Allen, M. (1982). *Listening: The forgotten skill.* New York: John Wiley.

Meek, A. (1999). *Communicating with the public - A guide for school leaders.* Alexandria, VA: Association for Supervision and Curriculum Development.

Williams, B. (1993). *More than 50 ways to build team consensus.* Palatine, IL: IRI/Skylight.

Principle 7: The Buck Stops Here

Positive Action: Be Consistent! Be Flexible! Be There!

Ackerman, R., Donaldson, G., & Van der Bogert, R. (1996). *Making sense as a school leader.* San Francisco: Jossey-Bass.

Stoltz, P. (1997). *Adversity quotient.* New York: John Wiley.

Torp, L., & Sage, S. (1998). *Problems as possibilities.* Alexandria, VA: Association for Supervision and Curriculum Development.

Principle 8: Together Is Better

Positive Action: Invite Partnerships!

Conference Board of Canada. 1996. *Business and Education Partnership Idea Book.* Available http://www.conferenceboard.ca/nbec

Craigen, J., & Ward, C. (1998). *What's this got to do with anything.* Ajax, Ontario, Canada: VISU TronX.

Dean, S. (2000). *Hearts and minds: A public school miracle.* Toronto, Canada: Viking Penguin Books.

Johnson, D., & Johnson, R. (1989). *Leading the co-operative school.* Edina, MN: Interaction Book Company.

Principle 9: Accountability Counts

Positive Action: Start Counting! Keep Counting!

Lezotte, L. (2001). *Effective schools.* Available: http://www.effectiveschools.com/free.stuff.html

Marzano, R. (2000). *Transforming classroom grading.* Alexandria, VA: Association for Supervision and Curriculum Development.

Sutton, R. (1997). *The learning school.* Salford, England: RS Publications.

Schmoker, M. (2000). *Results: The key to continuous school improvement.* Alexandria, VA: Association for Supervision and Curriculum Development.

Principle 10: Work Smarter.

Positive Action: Prioritize! Prioritize! Prioritize!

Anderson, G. (1995). *The 22 non-negotiable laws of wellness*. San Francisco: Harper.

Crawford, R. (1998). *How high can you bounce*. New York: Bantam Books.

Clemmer, J. (1999). *Growing the distance*. Kitchener, Canada: TCG Press.

O'Brien, R. (2001). *The resilient journey series*. Available: rdob@sympatico.ca

Posen, D. (1994). *Always change a losing game*. Toronto, Ontario, Canada: Key Porter Books.

Teachers Make x the Difference

The good teacher *instructs*

the excellent teacher *invites*

the superior teacher *involves*,

the great teacher *inspires*.

Robin Fogarty—Chicago, 1999